NCO

OLYMPIAD WORKBOOK

NATIONAL CYBER OLYMPIAD

- **01** Learning Objectives
- **02** Multiple Choice Questions
- **03** HOTS (Achievers Section)
- **04** Model Test Paper
- **05** Answer Keys and Solutions
- **06** OMR Answer Sheet

V&S PUBLISHERS

Published by:

V&S PUBLISHERS

F-2/16, Ansari road, Daryaganj, New Delhi-110002
☎ 23240026, 23240027 • *Fax:* 011-23240028
✉ info@vspublishers.com • ⊕ www.vspublishers.com

Online Brandstore: amazon.in/vspublishers

Regional Office : Hyderabad
5-1-707/1, Brij Bhawan (Beside Central Bank of India Lane)
Bank Street, Koti, Hyderabad - 500 095
☎ 040-24737290
✉ vspublishershyd@gmail.com

Follow us on:   

BUY OUR BOOKS FROM: AMAZON FLIPKART

© **Copyright:** *V&S* PUBLISHERS
ISBN 978-81-978176-2-5
New Edition

PUBLISHER'S NOTE

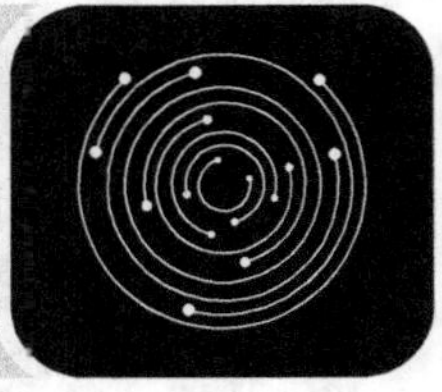

V&S Publishers has carved a significant niche in the publishing industry over the last decade, having successfully published more than 1000 titles across 9 languages spanning over 50 subject categories. Being known for the quality of content, we have built a reputation of excellence and reliability. We have consistently delivered **"Value & Substance"** to our readers, through a wide range of titles across a variety of genres covering school books, fiction and non-fiction that caters to different people from every section of the society.

The **Olympiad Guidebooks for classes 1-10** across all subjects, launched almost a decade ago, under the **GEN X Imprint**, became a go-to-source for the school students in no time, owing to their invaluable and substantive content written in a guidebook pattern,.

Having successfully sold a million copies of the same and in response to demand by both students as well as shopkeepers nationwide; we now present before you our newly launched **Olympiad Workbook Series**, designed for **classes 1-10 across 4 subjects**.

The workbooks are meticulously curated by a team of experienced educators, researchers and subject matter experts, edited by professionals and peer reviewed by teachers. The team has poured its efforts and expertise into creating a crisp and concise workbook which will help and guide the students to the path of success in Olympiad exams. The **MCQs** identified will not only help in scoring top marks in Olympiads but also inculcate a sense of deeper understanding of the subject, by way of solving **HOTS** and referring to complete solutions at the end of the book.

Here we present our new release– **OLYMPIAD WORKBOOK (NCO) CLASS–3** having following features:

- Based on the latest syllabi
- MCQs with comprehensive coverage of topics
- HOTS Questions liberally included
- A dedicated chapter on logical reasoning
- Model test paper for thorough practice
- Sample OMR sheet for real time simulation

We have made sure through our best efforts, that this workbook strictly follows the latest syllabi and patterns of the Olympiad Examination.

As **V&S Publishers** continuously strive to enhance the readability and maintain the credibility of our academic publications, we seek the support of our valuable readers in influencing and enriching the lives of future generations of students.

P.S. While every care has been taken to ensure the correctness of the content, if you come across any error, howsoever minor, do not hesitate to discuss with teachers while pointing that out to us in no uncertain terms.

We wish you all the best for your exams!

DISTINCTIVE FEATURES

CONTENTS

FUNDAMENTALS OF COMPUTER

LEARNING OBJECTIVES

➤ Monitor
➤ Input Devices
➤ Output Devices
➤ Storage Devices
➤ Memory

MULTIPLE CHOICE QUESTIONS

1. Which of the following is the image of an Abacus?

   (A)

   (B)

   (C)

   (D)

2. The first machine which had wheels and gears was ______.
   (A) Pascaline
   (B) Calculator
   (C) Punch Card
   (D) Difference Engine

3. Computer is derived from the word ______.
   (A) Storage
   (B) Compute
   (C) Calculate
   (D) Difference engine

4. The first machine computer was invented by ______.
   (A) Bill Gates
   (B) Charles Babbage
   (C) John Napier
   (D) Blaise Pascal

5. A CPU is called the ______ of computer.

   (A) 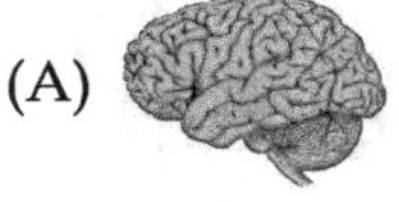   (B) 

   (C) 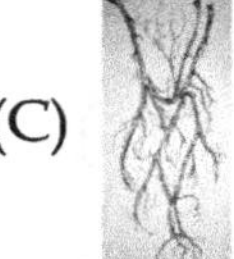   (D) 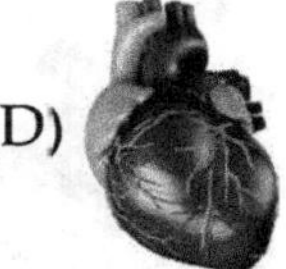

6. Where does a computer save its data?
   (A) Memory
   (B) Headphones
   (C) Mouse
   (D) A computer does not save its data.

7. This program controls the overall working of a computer. It is the ______.
   (A) Internet Explorer
   (B) MS-Paint
   (C) Operating system
   (D) VLC player

8. Which of the following devices is used to store information?

(A) 

(B) 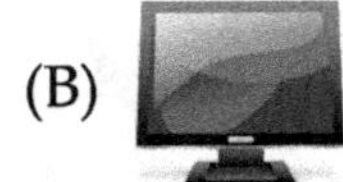

(C) 

(D) 

9. A computer is a powerful machine. Which of the following is NOT a feature of the computer?
   (A) High speed
   (B) High reliability
   (C) Huge storage
   (D) High cost

10. Which of the following CANNOT be used in a computer?

(A) 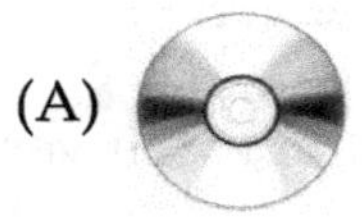

(B) 

(C) 

(D) 

11. This computer peripheral allows you to copy information from the computer screen to paper.

(A) 

(B) 

(C) 

(D) 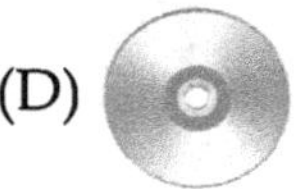

12. The full form of DVD is ________.
    (A) Disk Video Device
    (B) Digital Video Device
    (C) Digital Versatile Disk
    (D) Disk and Video Drum

13. These devices connect computer components so that they may communicate with each other. You often have more than one in a system.
    (A) Cables
    (B) Diskettes
    (C) Headphones
    (D) Keys

14. You can record your voice or other sounds into the computer when you speak over a ________.

(A) 

(B) 

(C) 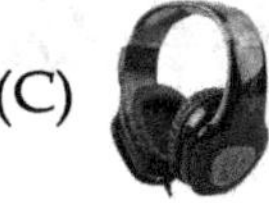

(D) 

15. Which of the following statements is incorrect with respect to computers in schools?
    (A) Used to maintain playgrounds
    (B) Used to prepare your result
    (C) Used in library to maintain records
    (D) Used to maintain information about teachers

16. In school, a computer is NOT used ______.
    (A) In computer lab
    (B) To make timetable
    (C) To prepare medical reports of patients
    (D) To store data

17. Which of the following statements is incorrect regarding the use of computer in banks?
    (A) Banks issue only debit cards.
    (B) Banks issue monthly account statements.
    (C) Banks keep details of money deposited and withdrawn.
    (D) None of these.

18. Computers are NOT used for billing in ________.
    (A) Malls and Shops
    (B) Restaurants and Hotels
    (C) Hospital and Pathologies
    (D) None of these

19. In hospitals, CAT Scan is very useful. What does CAT stand for?

   (A) Cathode and typing
   (B) Computer Auto Test
   (C) Computer Axial Test
   (D) Computer Axial Tomography

20. Which of the following options are correct uses of computers in schools?

   (i)   It can be used as a tutor.
   (ii) It is used for maintaining student details.
   (iii) It is used for diagnosing diseases.

   (A) Only (iii)
   (B) Only (ii) and (iii)
   (C) Only (i) and (ii)
   (D) All of these

HOTS (ACHIEVERS SECTION)

21. Identify the following.

   ■ It is a medium-sized digital computer that supports many users simultaneously.

   ■ Users can access this type of computer through their PCs.

   ■ These computers are used for real time applications.

   PDP 11, IBM (800 series) are examples of this type of computer.

   (A) Minicomputer
   (B) Microcomputer
   (C) Mainframe computer
   (D) Supercomputer

22. Which of the following is a microcomputer?

   1.

   2.

   3.

   4.

   (A) 1 and 3 only
   (B) 2 and 4 only
   (C) 1, 3 and 4 only
   (D) All of these

23. A computer is used for performing complex scientific calculations, for designing and making CAD CAM applications. It is also used for visualizing 3-D objects. The given information shows that a computer is used in __________.

   (A) School
   (B) Railways
   (C) Publishing
   (D) Science and Engineering

24. Which of the following options correctly describes the steps of the given diagram in the same order?

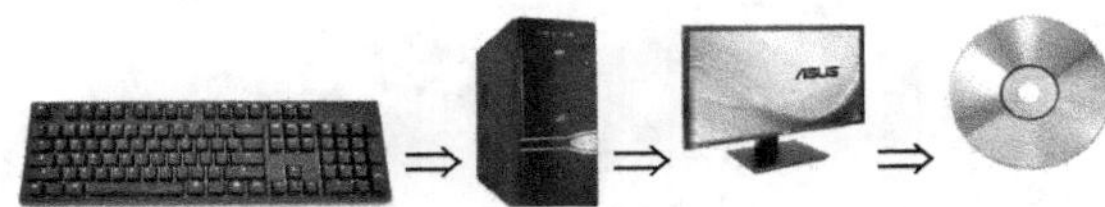

   (A) Computer accepts the input data, it processes the input data, output result is generated, output is then stored in a storage device
   (B) Computer processes input data, output is stored in storage device, it accepts input data, output result is generated
   (C) Computer accepts input data, output result is generated, it processes input data, output is stored in a storage device
   (D) Computer accepts input data, it processes input data, output is stored in storage device, output result is generated.

25. Which of the following devices will NOT be needed if you want to preview and print the the document?

(1)  (2)

(3) (4)

(A) Only 1
(B) Only 2
(C) Only 3 and 4
(D) 1, 3 and 4

1.	Ⓐ Ⓑ Ⓒ Ⓓ	6.	Ⓐ Ⓑ Ⓒ Ⓓ	11.	Ⓐ Ⓑ Ⓒ Ⓓ	16.	Ⓐ Ⓑ Ⓒ Ⓓ	21.	Ⓐ Ⓑ Ⓒ Ⓓ
2.	Ⓐ Ⓑ Ⓒ Ⓓ	7.	Ⓐ Ⓑ Ⓒ Ⓓ	12.	Ⓐ Ⓑ Ⓒ Ⓓ	17.	Ⓐ Ⓑ Ⓒ Ⓓ	22.	Ⓐ Ⓑ Ⓒ Ⓓ
3.	Ⓐ Ⓑ Ⓒ Ⓓ	8.	Ⓐ Ⓑ Ⓒ Ⓓ	13.	Ⓐ Ⓑ Ⓒ Ⓓ	18.	Ⓐ Ⓑ Ⓒ Ⓓ	23.	Ⓐ Ⓑ Ⓒ Ⓓ
4.	Ⓐ Ⓑ Ⓒ Ⓓ	9.	Ⓐ Ⓑ Ⓒ Ⓓ	14.	Ⓐ Ⓑ Ⓒ Ⓓ	19.	Ⓐ Ⓑ Ⓒ Ⓓ	24.	Ⓐ Ⓑ Ⓒ Ⓓ
5.	Ⓐ Ⓑ Ⓒ Ⓓ	10.	Ⓐ Ⓑ Ⓒ Ⓓ	15.	Ⓐ Ⓑ Ⓒ Ⓓ	20.	Ⓐ Ⓑ Ⓒ Ⓓ	25.	Ⓐ Ⓑ Ⓒ Ⓓ

OLYMPIAD WORKBOOK (NCO) CLASS— 3

INPUT AND OUTPUT DEVICES

2

LEARNING OBJECTIVES

➤ Different input devices in a computer
➤ Different output devices in a computer

MULTIPLE CHOICE QUESTIONS

1. Which among the following is a cursor control input device?

(A)

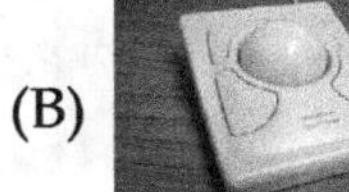

(B)

(C)

(D) None of these

2. ______ is the means of direct data entry into a computer. It is a small plastic device that is normally connected to a computer, it reads the data encoded on the card inserted into it and transfers its data to the computer for further processing.

(A) Scanner

(B) Plotter

(C) Electronic Card Reader

(D) Optical Mark Reader

3. The output displayed on ____ is known as a soft copy.

(A) Speakers

(B) Monitor

(C) Printer

(D) Scanner

4. Unscramble the word given here and select the device on which it is found.

LOSCRL LHEEW

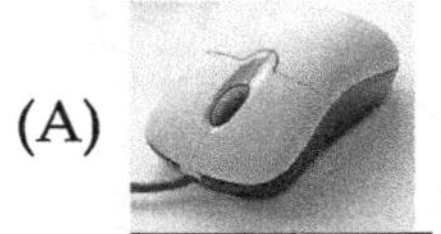

(A)

(B)

(C)

(D)

5. I am a device like a mouse. Instead of having a ball at the bottom, I have a ball at the top.

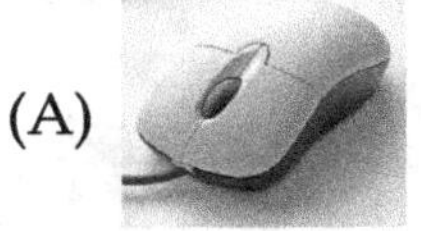

(A)

(B)

(C)

(D)

6. Select the INCORRECT match.

(A) **Caps Lock**

— A toggle key

(B) ⇧ Shift

— Used in combination with other keys for typing symbols

(C) **Tab**

— Used to move the cursor at the end of a document

(D) esc

— Used to cancel an operation

7. It reads pictures, words or numbers from a page directly and can change them into a form that a computer can understand. Identify it.

(A) 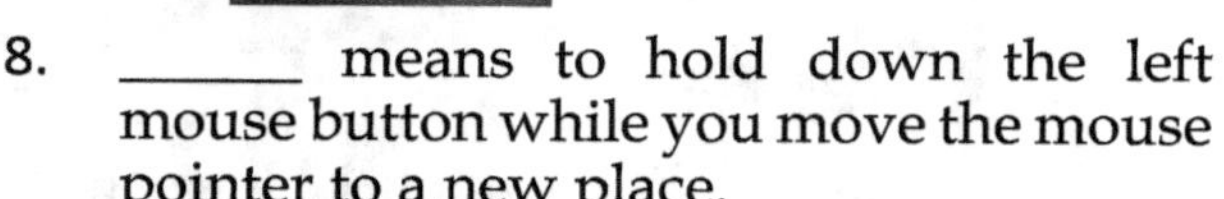   (B)

(C)   (D) None of these

8. ________ means to hold down the left mouse button while you move the mouse pointer to a new place.
(A) Single click   (B) Double click
(C) Dragging   (D) Left click

9. Select the odd one out.

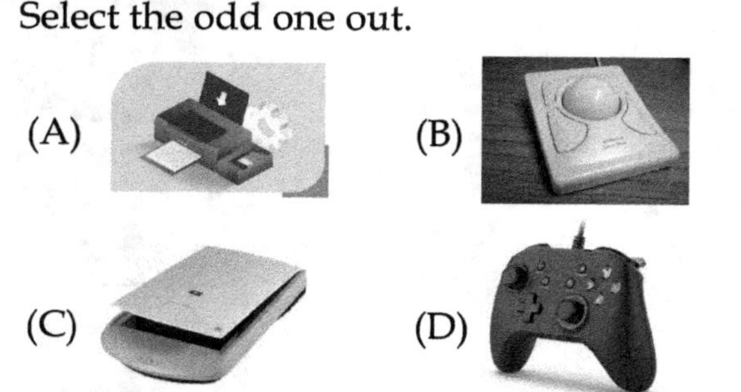

(A)   (B)

(C)   (D)

10. The image shown here is of an ______ device and it is a ____________.

(A) Input, Reader
(B) Output, LED Monitor
(C) Output, Scanner
(D) Input, CRT Machine

11. Pressing this key allows you to jump the cursor several spaces forward at once.

(A) **Caps Lock**

(B) spacebar.

(C) ⇧ Shift

(D) **Tab**

12. A wireless mouse ________.
(A) Needs to be connected with the computer with a USB cable
(B) Requires shorter cable than wired mouse
(C) Makes it easy to control the cursor from anywhere
(D) Both [A] and [B]

13. Which of the following printers is more suitable where continuous paper stationery is used?
(A) Dot matrix printers
(B) Daisy wheel printers
(C) Inkjet printers
(D) Laser printers

14. Select the CORRECT match.
    (A) The longest key on the keyboard -

    (B) Moves the cursor up, down, left or right -

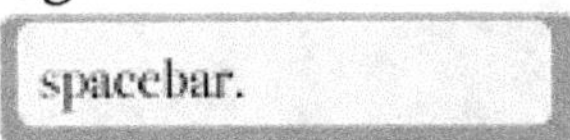

    (C) Erases the text to the right of cursor -

    (D) Changes the case of text -

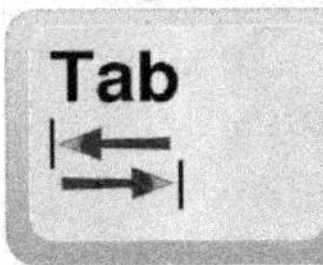

15. Which of the following devices is/are used to feed audio data in a computer?

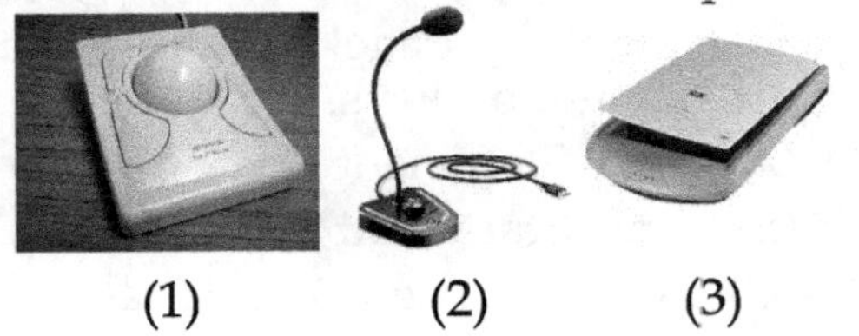

    (1)   (2)   (3)
    (A) Only (1)
    (B) Only (2)
    (C) Both (1) and (2)
    (D) Both (1) and (3)

16. Which of the following input devices is commonly found in laptops?
    (A) Joystick
    (B) Touchpad
    (C) Printer
    (D) Light Pen

17. Input and output devices are connected to the computer through the __________.
    (A) Monitor   (B) Keyboard
    (C) Port   (D) zRAM

18. It has characters printed on the keys and each press of a key corresponds to a single written symbol on the screen. Identify the device.
    (A) CPU
    (B) Mic
    (C) Keyboard
    (D) mouse

19. Select the INCORRECT statement.
    (A) Light pen and joystick are pointing devices.
    (B) OMR is a special type of scanner used to evaluate MCQ answer sheets.
    (C) Webcam is primarily used to give sound output.
    (D) Plotter is used for designing purposes.

20. Which device is commonly used in shopping malls and large retail stores?
    (A) Keyboard
    (B) Point of sale device
    (C) Touchscreen
    (D) Monitor

21. Which of the following statements hold(s) true about magnetic stripe reader?

    Statement 1: It is a data capture device.

    Statement 2: It reads information stored in credit or access control cards.

    (A) Only Statement 1
    (B) Only Statement 2
    (C) Both Statement 1 and Statement 2
    (D) Neither Statement 1 nor Statement 2

22. There is a multi-functioning device. It consists of a Printer, Scanner, Fax and Photocopier. From the following options, determine what kind of device is it?

    (A) Only input device
    (B) Only output device
    (C) Both input and output device
    (D) Central processing unit

23. Unscramble the given word and then select the statement(s) which is/are CORRECT. TJEKIN

    (1) The word when unscrambled forms the name of a printer.
    (2) It is a process by which computer operates on data.
    (3) It is a device found inside the motherboard.

    (A) Only (1)
    (B) Only (2)
    (C) Only (3)
    (D) Both (2) and (3)

24. Identify the device shown here and then select the purpose it is used for.

    (A) It is used to read some specially printed characters found on cheques.
    (B) A manual entry data device which looks like a typewriter.
    (C) A touchscreen device which acts as both input and output device.
    (D) A processing device found in desktop computers.

25. Which of the following statements hold(s) true about keys of keyboard?

    Statement 1: Ctrl, Alt and Shift keys appear twice on a standard keyboard.

    Statement 2: Page Up and Page down are navigation keys.

    (A) Only Statement 1
    (B) Only Statement 2
    (C) Both Statement 1 and Statement 2
    (D) Neither Statement 1 nor Statement 2

Darken Your Choice with HB Pencil

1.	Ⓐ Ⓑ Ⓒ Ⓓ	6.	Ⓐ Ⓑ Ⓒ Ⓓ	11.	Ⓐ Ⓑ Ⓒ Ⓓ	16.	Ⓐ Ⓑ Ⓒ Ⓓ	21.	Ⓐ Ⓑ Ⓒ Ⓓ
2.	Ⓐ Ⓑ Ⓒ Ⓓ	7.	Ⓐ Ⓑ Ⓒ Ⓓ	12.	Ⓐ Ⓑ Ⓒ Ⓓ	17.	Ⓐ Ⓑ Ⓒ Ⓓ	22.	Ⓐ Ⓑ Ⓒ Ⓓ
3.	Ⓐ Ⓑ Ⓒ Ⓓ	8.	Ⓐ Ⓑ Ⓒ Ⓓ	13.	Ⓐ Ⓑ Ⓒ Ⓓ	18.	Ⓐ Ⓑ Ⓒ Ⓓ	23.	Ⓐ Ⓑ Ⓒ Ⓓ
4.	Ⓐ Ⓑ Ⓒ Ⓓ	9.	Ⓐ Ⓑ Ⓒ Ⓓ	14.	Ⓐ Ⓑ Ⓒ Ⓓ	19.	Ⓐ Ⓑ Ⓒ Ⓓ	24.	Ⓐ Ⓑ Ⓒ Ⓓ
5.	Ⓐ Ⓑ Ⓒ Ⓓ	10.	Ⓐ Ⓑ Ⓒ Ⓓ	15.	Ⓐ Ⓑ Ⓒ Ⓓ	20.	Ⓐ Ⓑ Ⓒ Ⓓ	25.	Ⓐ Ⓑ Ⓒ Ⓓ

MS PAINT

3

LEARNING OBJECTIVES

➤ The Title Bar
➤ The Menu Bar

➤ Paint Button
➤ The Tools Menu

MULTIPLE CHOICE QUESTIONS

1. What is the area shown in the image called?

   (A) Ribbon Toolbar
   (B) Quick Access Toolbar
   (C) Menu Bar
   (D) Icon Toolbar

2. What happens when you click on the button pointed by the arrow?

   (A) The customized Quick Access Toolbar Menu is displayed.
   (B) List of all paints is displayed.
   (C) The Zoom in option is displayed.
   (D) The main menu of MS Paint is displayed.

3. Match the following.

   Column-I   Column-II

   (i)   (A) To draw a perfect circle.

   (ii) ○   (B) To make free hand drawing.

   (iii) ✏   (C) To add a little text to your drawing.

   (iv) **A**   (D) To fill an area with the current color.

   (A) (i)–(D), (ii)–(A), (iii)–(B), (iv)–(C)
   (B) (i)–(D), (ii)–(A), (iii)–(C), (iv)–(B)
   (C) (i)–(A), (ii)–(D), (iii)–(C), (iv)–(B)
   (D) (i)–(A), (ii)–(C), (iii)–(B), (iv)–(D)

4. To select the entire drawing, using the keyboard press ______.

   (A) Ctrl + A
   (B) Ctrl + W
   (C) Ctrl + D
   (D) Ctrl + M

5. The ________ version of MS Paint makes use of the Ribbon UI.
   (A) Windows 7
   (B) Windows 98
   (C) Windows Vista
   (D) Windows XP

6. Why is working with text sometimes difficult in MS Paint?
   (A) You cannot read your text.
   (B) Once you add text and click off it, you cannot edit it or change the font or size.
   (C) You cannot change the size of the text.
   (D) You cannot change the font.

7. If Sheetal wants to use the exact same colour she used previously, the best way to select that colour is to use _______.

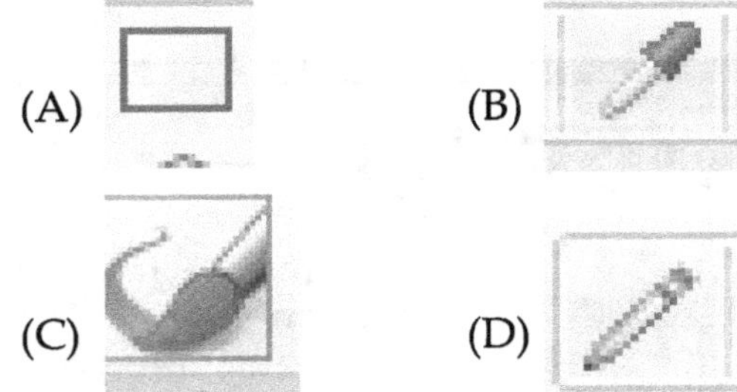

   (A)   (B)

   (C)   (D)

8. The colour boxes shown in this image are found in the _______.

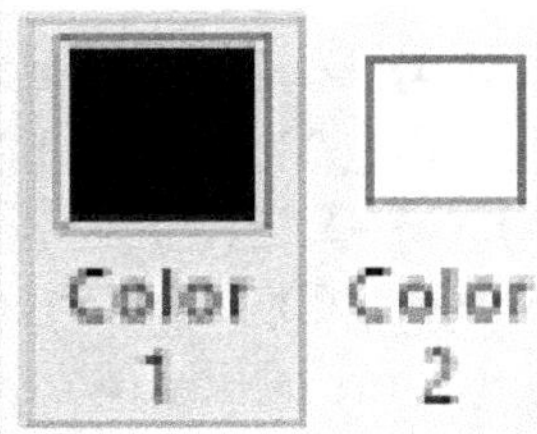

   (A) View tab of the Ribbon
   (B) Quick Access Toolbar
   (C) Colour Palette
   (D) Home tab of the Ribbon

9. Given below are the steps to draw a perfect square in MS Paint. However while writing the process, the steps got jumped. Help us arrange the steps in the correct order.
   (i) Drag the mouse pointer diagonally.
   (ii) Move the mouse pointer to the drawing area.
   (iii) Release the ⇧ Shift

(iv) Press ⇧ Shift

(v) Release the mouse button.

(vi) Select the ☐ tool.

(vii) Click in the drawing area.
   (A) (vii) – (iii) – (iv) – (v) – (i) – (vi) – (ii)
   (B) (vii) – (vi) – (v) – (i) – (ii) – (iii) – (iv)
   (C) (vi) – (ii) – (vii) – (iv) – (i) – (v) – (iii)
   (D) (i) – (ii) – (iii) – (iv) – (vii) – (vi) – (v)

10. Under the Home tab, in the Colours group, when you click Colour 1 and then click a colour square, what happens?
    (A) It changes the background colour of the drawing.
    (B) It changes the foreground colour selection.
    (C) It changes the background colour selection.
    (D) It changes the foreground colour of the drawing.

11. Which operation in MS Paint would change the image X to image Y?

Image X   **Image Y**

    (A) Rotate by 180°
    (B) Flip vertical
    (C) Flip horizontal
    (D) Rotate Right 90°

12. Which operation in MS Paint would change the Image X to the Image Y?

Image X   **Image Y**

    (A) Flip vertical
    (B) Skew
    (C) Rotate 180°
    (D) Flip horizontal

13. Which MS Paint tool can be used to create the image?

OLYMPIAD WORKBOOK (NCO) CLASS– 3

(A) 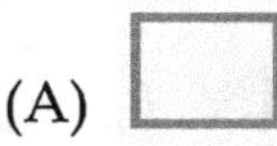   (B) 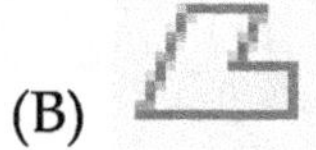

(C) 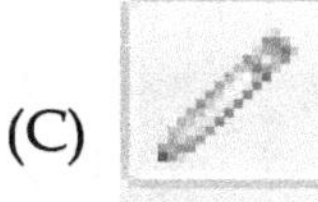   (D) 

14. The hot key sequence to view, hide and use ruler is _______.

(A) Ctrl + E

(B) Ctrl + W

(C) Ctrl + R

(D) Ctrl + I

15. Identify the icon used to make shapes shown here.

(A) Rounded cloud callout
(B) Rectangular callout
(C) Oval callout
(D) Cloud callout

16. Which operation in MS Paint would change the Image X to Image Y?

Image X   **Image Y**

(A) Flip vertical   (B) Skew
(C) Rotate 180°   (D) Flip horizontal

17. 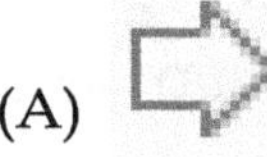 is used to _______.

(A) Magnify the current drawing
(B) Display the current drawing in full screen
(C) Save a picture for the first time
(D) Zoom in and Zoom Out the current drawing

18. Which of the following is NOT a ready made shape in MS Paint?

(A) 

(B) 

(C) 

(D)

19. The hot key sequence to 'Resize and Skew' the picture or selection is _______.
(A) Ctrl + R
(B) Ctrl + W
(C) Ctrl + G
(D) Ctrl + I

20. While working on a wide picture in MS Paint, which of the following options would you use to move the picture left or right to see the extreme side edges?
(A) Horizontal scroll bar
(B) Status bar
(C) Vertical scroll bar
(D) Ribbon toolbar

21. While drawing a curved line, you must use a _______.

(A) 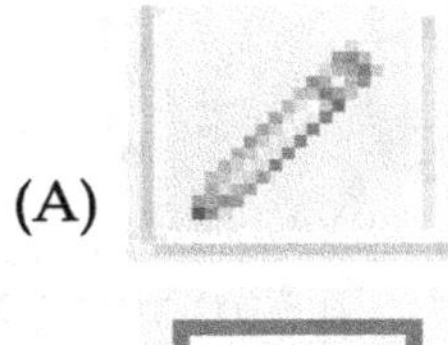

(B) 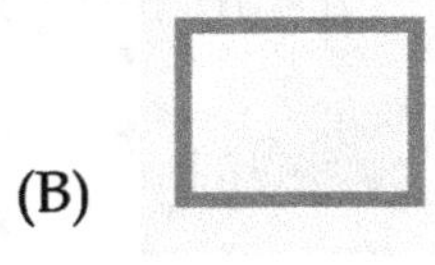

(C) 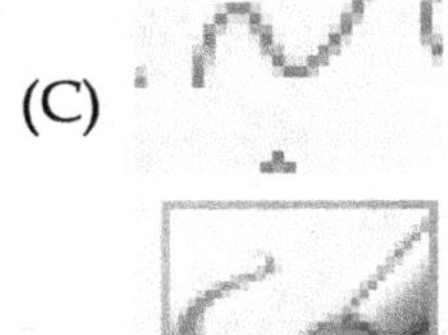

(D) 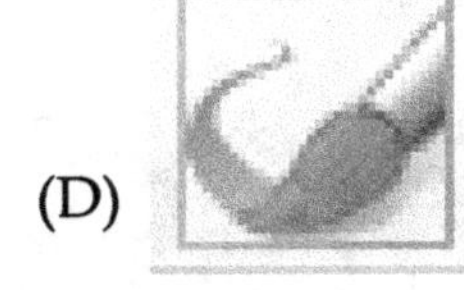

22. Which of the following is NOT a feature of MS Paint?
    (A) It can be used to create, edit and print pictures.
    (B) It can be used to draw pictures, cartoons, maps, & subject material.
    (C) It can be used to write and edit letters and e-mails.
    (D) It can be used to view and edit scanned pictures.

23. To set the amount of white space in which you have to work, you should go to _______.

(A) Paint button 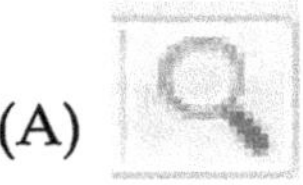 → Properties

(B) Paint button →  Page Setup

(C) Image → Resize

(D) Image → Resize and Skew

24. To zoom an object in or out, which tool will you use?

(A) 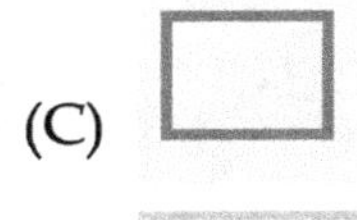

(B) 

(C)

(D)

25. Which of the following is NOT a way to clear your document of all work?

(A) Select the area with, ☐ then press _______

(B) Select the area with ☐, then press cut.

(C) Image → Select →

(D) Image →

26. Find the odd one out.

(A) 

(B)

(C)

(D)

27. The two figures are drawn in MS Paint of Windows 7 using the pencil tool. Which of the following keyboard shortcuts is used to increase the width of the pencil tool in figure 2?

Figure 1   Figure 2

(A) Ctrl + [+] key
(B) Ctrl + [+/=] key
(C) Ctrl + [*/8] key
(D) Ctrl + ↑

28. In text tools tab, the given two options come under which group of MS Paint of Windows 7 when text tool is selected?

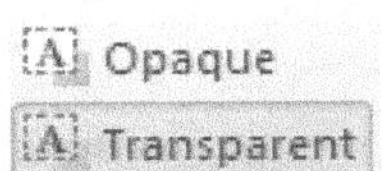

(A) Font   (B) Background
(C) Colours   (D) Clipboard

29. Fill in the blanks:
   1. In paint brush application you __________ cut or remove any portion of the picture or drawing.
   2. __________ is used for spraying the colour.
   3. __________ tool to draw thin, free form lines or curves.

   (A) Cannot, Brush, Pen
   (B) Can, Airbrush, Pencil
   (C) Should not, Dropper, Pencil
   (D) Should, Container, Sketch

30. Drawing on a computer is difficult activity for Lina. Actually she wants to draw a smooth and curve line for her project on a computer. But she does not know how to do it? Which one of the following tool she should use to do the same?

   (A) Line tool   (B) Curve tool
   (C) Smooth tool   (D) Circle tool

Darken Your Choice with HB Pencil

1.	Ⓐ Ⓑ Ⓒ Ⓓ	7.	Ⓐ Ⓑ Ⓒ Ⓓ	13.	Ⓐ Ⓑ Ⓒ Ⓓ	19.	Ⓐ Ⓑ Ⓒ Ⓓ	25.	Ⓐ Ⓑ Ⓒ Ⓓ
2.	Ⓐ Ⓑ Ⓒ Ⓓ	8.	Ⓐ Ⓑ Ⓒ Ⓓ	14.	Ⓐ Ⓑ Ⓒ Ⓓ	20.	Ⓐ Ⓑ Ⓒ Ⓓ	26.	Ⓐ Ⓑ Ⓒ Ⓓ
3.	Ⓐ Ⓑ Ⓒ Ⓓ	9.	Ⓐ Ⓑ Ⓒ Ⓓ	15.	Ⓐ Ⓑ Ⓒ Ⓓ	21.	Ⓐ Ⓑ Ⓒ Ⓓ	27.	Ⓐ Ⓑ Ⓒ Ⓓ
4.	Ⓐ Ⓑ Ⓒ Ⓓ	10.	Ⓐ Ⓑ Ⓒ Ⓓ	16.	Ⓐ Ⓑ Ⓒ Ⓓ	22.	Ⓐ Ⓑ Ⓒ Ⓓ	28.	Ⓐ Ⓑ Ⓒ Ⓓ
5.	Ⓐ Ⓑ Ⓒ Ⓓ	11.	Ⓐ Ⓑ Ⓒ Ⓓ	17.	Ⓐ Ⓑ Ⓒ Ⓓ	23.	Ⓐ Ⓑ Ⓒ Ⓓ	29.	Ⓐ Ⓑ Ⓒ Ⓓ
6.	Ⓐ Ⓑ Ⓒ Ⓓ	12.	Ⓐ Ⓑ Ⓒ Ⓓ	18.	Ⓐ Ⓑ Ⓒ Ⓓ	24.	Ⓐ Ⓑ Ⓒ Ⓓ	30.	Ⓐ Ⓑ Ⓒ Ⓓ

INTRODUCTION TO INTERNET

LEARNING OBJECTIVES

➤ Online and Offline

MULTIPLE CHOICE QUESTIONS

1. What is the World Wide Web?
   (A) A computer game
   (B) A software program
   (C) The part of the internet that enables information sharing via interconnected pages
   (D) Another name for the Internet

2. What is the best way to find information on a website?
   (A) E-mails
   (B) Search engines
   (C) Newsgroups
   (D) Discussion groups

3. The Internet was originally developed by ______.
   (A) Computer hackers
   (B) Internet corporation
   (C) The U.S. Department of Defense
   (D) The University of Michigan

4. Which description does NOT apply to the Internet?
   (A) An interconnected system of networks that allows for communication through e-mail and the World Wide Web.
   (B) A public network neither owned nor run by any one group or individual.
   (C) A vast network that connects millions of computers around the world.
   (D) A catalogue of information organized and fact checked by a governing body.

5. Which of the following is a search engine?
   (A) Macromedia Flash
   (B) Google
   (C) Netscape
   (D) Librarian's Index to the Internet

6. What is a URL?
   (A) A computer software program
   (B) A type of UFO
   (C) The address of a document or "page" on the World Wide Web
   (D) An acronym for Ultimate Resources for Learning

7. http://www.shraddhasingh.com is an example of a/an ______.
   (A) URL
   (B) Access code
   (C) Directory
   (D) Server

8. A single document on the internet is called a/an ______.
   (A) E-mail
   (B) Website
   (C) Webpage
   (D) None of these

9. A collection of linked documents that contains text and other media elements, such as graphics, animation, video and audio is ______.
   (A) Webpage
   (B) E-mail
   (C) Website
   (D) Search Engine

10. A program that searches for web documents with keywords you specify.
    (A) Search Engine
    (B) E-mail
    (C) Website
    (D) Folder

11. What do you mean by online?
    (A) When you are connected to the internet through an ISP or a network
    (B) When you yourself go on the internet
    (C) When you are connected to a telephone
    (D) None of these

12. The full form of ISP is ______
    (A) Internet Search Provider
    (B) Internet Service Provider
    (C) Internet School Provider
    (D) Internet Shopping Provider

13. Which of the following is NOT required to connect to the Internet?
    (A) Search Engine
    (B) An account with the Internet Service Provider
    (C) Modem and Telephone connection
    (D) Computer

14. What is an Internet?
    (A) It is a global network.
    (B) It connects millions of computers.
    (C) The computers may be in the same office or geographically spread.
    (D) All of these

15. The image shown here is helpful in connecting to the internet. What is the device called?

    (A) Walky-talky
    (B) Telephone
    (C) Modem
    (D) Radio

16. On opening a browser, we see www. in the address bar of the browser. What does www stand for?
    (A) World Wide Word
    (B) Web Wide Word
    (C) Wide Web Word
    (D) World Wide Web

17. Which of the following is NOT a web browser?

(A) Mozilla Firefox 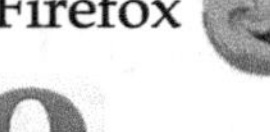

(B) Opera

(C) Google

(D) Internet Explorer

18. In the image given below, which is the address bar of the browser?

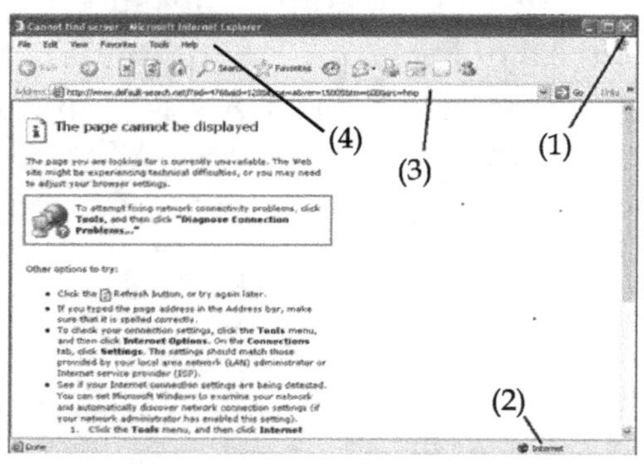

(A) (1)

(B) (2)

(C) (3)

(D) (4)

19. Connected computers in a __________ get their resources from a common source called __________ which are also a type of a computer.

(A) Network, Server
(B) Server, Network
(C) Server, UPS
(D) Network, UPS

20. What is the full form of URL?

(A) Universal Resource Log
(B) Unimportant Region Locator
(C) Universe of Resource Locations
(D) Uniform Resource Locator

HOTS (ACHIEVERS SECTION)

21. Identify the type of basic service with the help of information given.

- It enables a group of internet users belonging to a group to exchange their views on some common topic of interest.
- Comp.security.misk is an example of it that consists of users having interest in computer security issues.

(A) FTP
(B) Electronic
(C) Usenet
(D) Telnet

22. The site wikipedia.org provides an __________ and the site wiktionary.org provides an __________.

(A) Online dictionary, online encyclopedia
(B) Online encyclopedia, online dictionary
(C) Online news, online video
(D) Online songs, online video

23. Find the odd one out.

(A) Amazon
(B) Skype
(C) ooVoo
(D) Hangout

24. Select the odd one out.

(A) 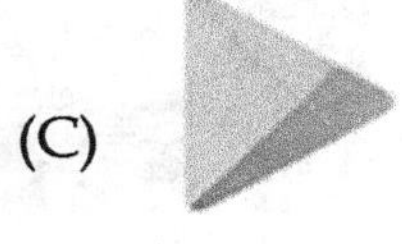

(B) **MobiKwik**

(C) Google Play

(D) *PayPal*

(A) To browse websites.

(B) To transfer data from one place to another.

(C) To provide a user interface.

(D) To search information.

25. For which of the following reason telephone connection is required to connect to the Internet?

1.	Ⓐ Ⓑ Ⓒ Ⓓ	6.	Ⓐ Ⓑ Ⓒ Ⓓ	11.	Ⓐ Ⓑ Ⓒ Ⓓ	16.	Ⓐ Ⓑ Ⓒ Ⓓ	21.	Ⓐ Ⓑ Ⓒ Ⓓ
2.	Ⓐ Ⓑ Ⓒ Ⓓ	7.	Ⓐ Ⓑ Ⓒ Ⓓ	12.	Ⓐ Ⓑ Ⓒ Ⓓ	17.	Ⓐ Ⓑ Ⓒ Ⓓ	22.	Ⓐ Ⓑ Ⓒ Ⓓ
3.	Ⓐ Ⓑ Ⓒ Ⓓ	8.	Ⓐ Ⓑ Ⓒ Ⓓ	13.	Ⓐ Ⓑ Ⓒ Ⓓ	18.	Ⓐ Ⓑ Ⓒ Ⓓ	23.	Ⓐ Ⓑ Ⓒ Ⓓ
4.	Ⓐ Ⓑ Ⓒ Ⓓ	9.	Ⓐ Ⓑ Ⓒ Ⓓ	14.	Ⓐ Ⓑ Ⓒ Ⓓ	19.	Ⓐ Ⓑ Ⓒ Ⓓ	24.	Ⓐ Ⓑ Ⓒ Ⓓ
5.	Ⓐ Ⓑ Ⓒ Ⓓ	10.	Ⓐ Ⓑ Ⓒ Ⓓ	15.	Ⓐ Ⓑ Ⓒ Ⓓ	20.	Ⓐ Ⓑ Ⓒ Ⓓ	25.	Ⓐ Ⓑ Ⓒ Ⓓ

MS WORD

LEARNING OBJECTIVES

➤ Quick Access Toolbar
➤ Function Tabs

MULTIPLE CHOICE QUESTIONS

Direction (1-2): Look at the given MS Word windows and answer the questions that follow.

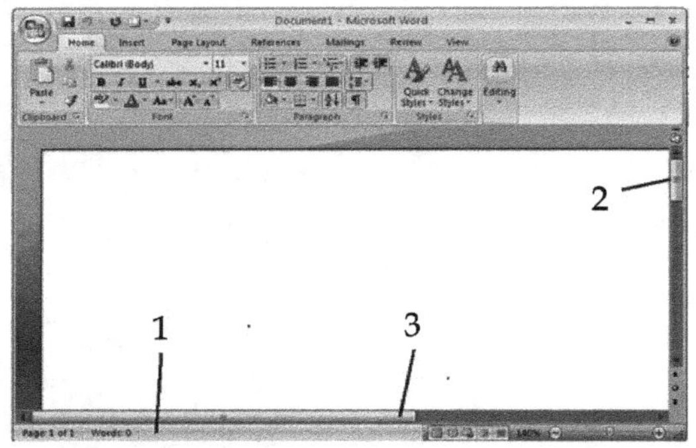

1. In the above window, what is the name of the area indicated by '2' and '3'?
   (A) Standard ribbon
   (B) Status Bar
   (C) Vertical and Horizontal Scroll Bar
   (D) Menu Bar

2. What label should be given for the area marked '1'?
   (A) Task bar   (B) Title bar
   (C) Scroll bar   (D) Status bar

3. Clicking on _________ changes the width from the left of the paper to where the text is displayed.
   (A) ≣   (B) ⋮≣
   (C) ⋮≣   (D) 🗐

4. When printing a Word document, click on the ______.
   (A) Page Layout tab of the ribbon and click 🖶
   (B) Click 🖶 on the Home Tab of the ribbon
   (C) Click 🖶 on the Quick Access Toolbar
   (D) Click on the view button to print.

5. If you make a mistake while typing or editing a Word document, you can undo your mistake by using ______.
   (A) 🖶   (B) ✂
   (C) 📋   (D) ↩

6. The number of pages to print per sheet can be changed from ______.
   (A) Using Page setup in the page Layout tab of the ribbon
   (B) 1 Page Per Sheet list in settings in the Printer Preview screen

(C) Setting the Number of pages to print in the Print dialog

(D) None of these

7. Predefined set of formatting options that have been named and saved are called __________.

(A) Styles   (B) Formal
(C) View   (D) Toolbar

8. Font size is measured in ______.

(A) Inches
(B) Centimeters
(C) Pixels
(D) Points

9. The key sequence used to select the entire document is ______.

(A) CTRL + A

(B) Ctrl + E

(C) Ctrl + Z

(D) Ctrl + R

10. What command removes the text from the document and places it in the clipboard?

(A) [image]   (B) [image]

(C) [image]   (D) [image]

11. The Home tab of the ribbon is used to ______.

(A) Print a document
(B) Change font size, alignments and styles in a document
(C) Insert pictures and shapes in the document
(D) View the Header and Footer in the document

12. How to select the entire paragraph in a document?

(A) Double click inside the paragraph.
(B) Single click inside the paragraph.
(C) Enter, single click and press enter.
(D) Triple click inside the paragraph.

13. To show the content not visible on the screen currently, ______.

(A) Add more text to the document
(B) Decrease the height of the page
(C) Increase the length of the page
(D) Scroll and bring the hidden parts of the document into the screen

14. What does this picture show?

(A) Start Menu   (B) Colour Menu
(C) Font Menu   (D) File Menu

15. Word Wrap is ________.

(A) When a Word is detected because it is too long to fit on a line
(B) When Word hyphenates a word at the end of a line
(C) When Word determines if there is room for a word at the end of a line or if it must go on the next line
(D) When the typist determines if there is room for word at the end of a line or it must go on the next line

16. Match the following.

Column-I	Column-II
(i)	(A) Increase Indent
(ii)	(B) Multilevel list
(iii)	(C) Bullets
(iv)	(D) Numbering
(v)	(e) Decrease Indent

(A) (i) – (A), (ii) – (B), (iii) – (C), (iv) – (D),
(v) – (e)

(B) (i) – (C), (ii) – (D), (iii) – (e), (iv) – (B),
(v) – (A)

(C) (i) – (C), (ii) – (D), (iii) – (B), (iv) – (e),
(v) – (A)

(D) (i) – (C), (ii) – (A), (iii) – (B), (iv) – (e),
(v) – (D)

17. The function of the given icon is ____________.

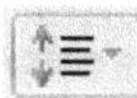

(A) Create small letters below text baseline

(B) Draw a line through the middle of the selected text

(C) Decrease font size

(D) Centre text

18. The file creator in MS Word 2010 has _________ extension.

(A) .doc

(B) .docx

(C) .dot

(D) .wri

19. Match the following.

Column-I   **Column-II**

(i) [icon]   (A) Format Painter

(ii) [icon]   (B) Shading

(iii) [icon]   (C) Clear Formatting

(iv) [icon]   (D) Text Highlight Colour

(A) (i) – (D), (ii) – (A), (iii) – (B), (iv) – (C)
(B) (i) – (D), (ii) – (A), (iii) – (C), (iv) – (B)
(C) (i) – (A), (ii) – (D), (iii) – (C), (iv) – (B)
(D) (i) – (A), (ii) – (C), (iii) – (B), (iv) – (D)

20. Match the following.

Column-I   **Column-II**

(i) Save a file   (A) CTRL + C

(ii) Italicize word or selected text   (B) Ctrl + S

(iii) Undo the last operation   (C) Ctrl + I

(iv) Copy selected text to clipboard   (D) Ctrl + Z

(A) (i) – (B), (ii) – (A), (iii) – (C), (iv) – (D)
(B) (i) – (B), (ii) – (C), (iii) – (D), (iv) – (A)
(C) (i) – (A), (ii) – (D), (iii) – (C), (iv) – (B)
(D) (i) – (B), (ii) – (C), (iii) – (A), (iv) – (D)

HOTS (ACHIEVERS SECTION)

21. Which of the following statements is INCORRECT regarding the given icon in MS Word 2010?

[icon]

(A) It comes under Home tab.

(B) It comes under Paragraph group.

(C) It is used to change the text colour.

(D) It changes the spacing between lines of text.

22. When you double click this [icon] icon in MS Word 2010, it _________________

(A) Closes the current window

(B) Leaves only the plain text

(C) Copies formatting from one place and applies it to another

(D) Shows paragraph marks

23. Which of the following steps is correct to insert a picture in MS Word 2010?

(A) Insert tab → illustrations group → click [icon] → Select file name in Insert Picture dialog box → click insert

(B) Hometab → illustrations group → click [icon] → Select file name in Insert Picture dialog box → click Insert

(C) Picture tab → illustration group → click [icon] → Select file name in Insert Picture dialog box → click Insert

(D) Both (A) and (B)

24. Given here is an image of options available in the Clipboard group of Home tab. Which of the following tasks is NOT possible with the help of these options?

(A) Removing a line of text
(B) Copying a line of text

(C) Repeating the last operation
(D) Pasting a copied part

25. Which of the following statements hold(s) true with respect to save as Save As commands?

Statement 1: Save command writes all the changes to the same file.

Statement 2: Save As command allows you to save all the changes to file using different name.

(A) Only Statement 1
(B) Only Statement 2
(C) Both Statement 1 and Statement 2
(D) Neither Statement 1 nor Statement 2

LEARNING OBJECTIVES

➤ Generations of Computer

MULTIPLE CHOICE QUESTIONS

1. The first computer programmer was __________.
   - (A) Charles Babbage
   - (B) Lady Ada Lovelace
   - (C) Bill Gates
   - (D) Seymour

2. What is the name of the device invented by John Napier?
   - (A) Napier's Bones
   - (A) Napier's Stones
   - (C) Napier's Rods
   - (D) Napier's Beads

3. Windows 7 is an example of __________.
   - (A) TUI Operating System
   - (B) Application Software
   - (C) GUI Operating System
   - (D) Software utility

4. Which of the following may destroy information on a computer?
   - (A) Bacteria
   - (B) Virus
   - (C) Backup
   - (D) Programs

5. Which of the following is/are present on the taskbar?
   - (A) Start button
   - (B) Notification Area
   - (C) System clock
   - (D) All of these

6. An arrow that is controlled by a mouse without using the keyboard is called __________.
   - (A) Pointer
   - (B) Chip
   - (C) Byte
   - (D) None of these

7. Which of the following is an incorrect e-mail address?
   - (A) shraddha.singh@gmail.com
   - (B) Shraddha.Singh@gmail.com
   - (C) Shraddha.Singh.gmail@com
   - (D) ShraddhaSingh@gmail.com

8. Which of following statements is correct?
   - (A) You tell the computer what to do by pressing the keys on the keyboard.
   - (B) Scanner cannot read words.
   - (C) Mouse does not point towards the items displayed.
   - (D) None of these

9. How do you open an icon on your desktop?

(A) Click the icon

(B) Right click the icon

(C) Double-click the icon

(D) Drag the icon

10. Match the following.

Column-I		Column-II
(i)	Sabeer Bhatia	(A) Sun Microsystems
(ii)	Vinod Khosla	(B) QWERTY keyboard layout
(iii)	Christopher Latham Sholes	(C) Pentium Chip
(iv)	Vinod Dham	(D) Hotmail

(A) (i)–(A), (ii)–(C), (iii)–(B), (iv)–(D)

(B) (i)–(D), (ii)–(C), (iii)–(B), (iv)–(A)

(C) (i)–(C), (ii)–(A), (iii)–(D), (iv)–(B)

(D) (i)–(D), (ii)–(A), (iii)–(B), (iv)–(C)

11. Select the incorrect match.

Column-I		Column-II
(A)	Produces the desired results	(i) Output
(B)	Processes the data according to given instructions	(ii) Processing
(C)	It holds CPU and memory	(iii) Motherboard
(D)	Inventor of QWERTY keyboard layout	(iv) Douglas Engelbart

Direction (12–19): View the given picture and answer the questions that follow.

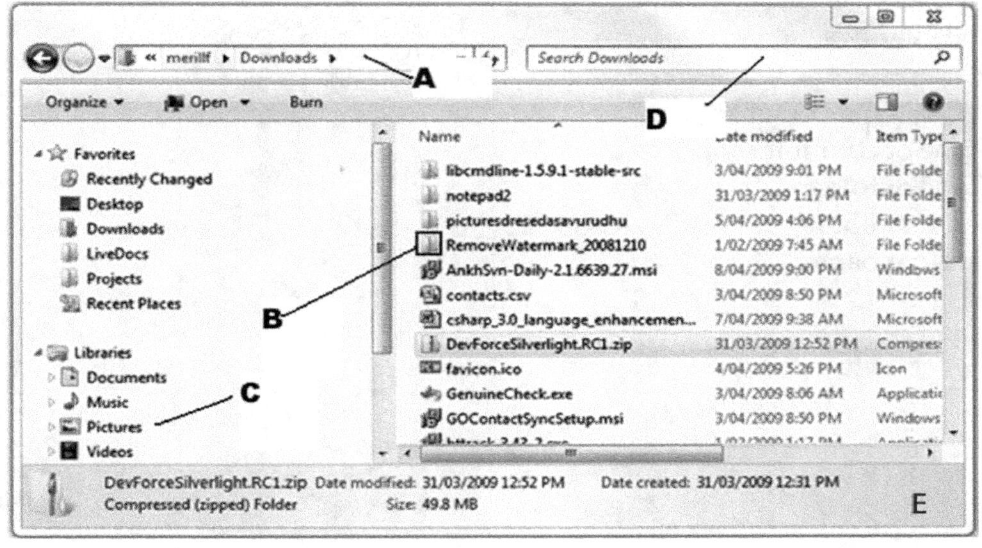

12. What is shown in the image here?

(A) The Windows Explorer

(B) The Internet Explorer

(C) The Disk Explorer

(D) The Data Explorer

13. What happens when you double click on the highlighted icon?

(A) The icon 'diagnostics' is selected and you can give a new name to it.

(B) The program 'diagnostics' is executed on the system.

(C) The file 'diagnostics' is opened in a Word processor.

(D) The folder 'diagnostics' is opened and the files in that folder are displayed.

14. The image indicated by the letter (B) is an example of a ______.
    (A) Button
    (B) File icon
    (C) Folder icon
    (D) Status icon

15. The area indicated by letter (E) is an example of ______ pane.
    (A) Navigation
    (B) Details
    (C) Preview
    (D) Tiles

16. When you click on the panel marked by (A) in figure, what will be displayed in the panel?
    (A) You cannot click on the panel
    (B) C:\Users\merilf\Downloads
    (C) C:\Windows
    (D) D:\

17. What does (C) represent?
    (A) Name of computer
    (B) Name of folder
    (C) Name of library
    (D) Random name

18. What is shown by (D) in the image?
    (A) It is the search panel used to search files and folders in the current folder.
    (B) It is the browser address bar. You can enter the name of the website to go there.
    (C) Both (A) and (B)
    (D) None of these

19. What does (D) represent?
    (A) Preview
    (B) Get help
    (C) Change view
    (D) Search

20. You click on which of the following buttons to close a window?

(A) 

(B) 

(C) 

(D) 

21. The list of computing technology that had arrived before the development of first generation computers is given below. Arrange them in increasing order of their arrivals.

    i.   Abacus
    ii. Pascaline
    iii. Napier's Bones
    iv. Stepped Reckoner
    v.   Babbage's analytical engine

    (A) i, ii, iii, iv, v   (B) i, iii, ii, iv, v
    (C) ii, iii, i, iv, v   (D) iv, v, iii, ii, i

22. Fill in the blanks

    i.   ______ refers to that the part of the computer which can both be touched and seen.
    ii. Design and implementation of software varies depending on the complexity of the ______.
    iii. ______ makes the hardware function properly and to an optimum level.

    (A) Software, hardware and software
    (B) Hardware, software and software
    (C) Motherboard, hardware and software
    (D) Hardware, software and hardware

23. Which among the following registers is loaded with the contents of the memory location pointed by the PC?
    (A) Memory address registers
    (B) Memory data registers
    (C) Instruction register
    (D) Program counter

24. Which 8-bit chip was used in many of today's TRS-80 computers?
    (A) Z-8000
    (B) Motorola 6809
    (C) Z-8808
    (D) Z-80

25. ULSI stands for?
    (A) Ultra Large Scale Integration
    (B) Under Lower Scale Integration
    (C) Ultra Lower Scale Integration
    (D) Under Large Scale Integration

1.	Ⓐ Ⓑ Ⓒ Ⓓ	6.	Ⓐ Ⓑ Ⓒ Ⓓ	11.	Ⓐ Ⓑ Ⓒ Ⓓ	16.	Ⓐ Ⓑ Ⓒ Ⓓ	21.	Ⓐ Ⓑ Ⓒ Ⓓ
2.	Ⓐ Ⓑ Ⓒ Ⓓ	7.	Ⓐ Ⓑ Ⓒ Ⓓ	12.	Ⓐ Ⓑ Ⓒ Ⓓ	17.	Ⓐ Ⓑ Ⓒ Ⓓ	22.	Ⓐ Ⓑ Ⓒ Ⓓ
3.	Ⓐ Ⓑ Ⓒ Ⓓ	8.	Ⓐ Ⓑ Ⓒ Ⓓ	13.	Ⓐ Ⓑ Ⓒ Ⓓ	18.	Ⓐ Ⓑ Ⓒ Ⓓ	23.	Ⓐ Ⓑ Ⓒ Ⓓ
4.	Ⓐ Ⓑ Ⓒ Ⓓ	9.	Ⓐ Ⓑ Ⓒ Ⓓ	14.	Ⓐ Ⓑ Ⓒ Ⓓ	19.	Ⓐ Ⓑ Ⓒ Ⓓ	24.	Ⓐ Ⓑ Ⓒ Ⓓ
5.	Ⓐ Ⓑ Ⓒ Ⓓ	10.	Ⓐ Ⓑ Ⓒ Ⓓ	15.	Ⓐ Ⓑ Ⓒ Ⓓ	20.	Ⓐ Ⓑ Ⓒ Ⓓ	25.	Ⓐ Ⓑ Ⓒ Ⓓ

LATEST DEVELOPMENTS IN 'IT'

LEARNING OBJECTIVES

➤ Whatsapp and Viber

MULTIPLE CHOICE QUESTIONS

1. Which is the Windows Operating System released on October 17, 2013?
   (A) Windows 7
   (B) Windows 8.1
   (C) Windows 2013
   (D) Windows 10

2. MS Office 2013 is suitable for ______ and ______ systems.
   (A) IA-32
   (B) X 64
   (C) X65
   (D) Both (A) and (B)

3. Which is the logo of MS Word 2013?
   (A)
   (B)
   (C)
   (D)

4. The iPad is developed and marketed by ________.

   (A) Google (B) ![Apple]
   (C) SAMSUNG (D) NOKIA Connecting People

5. Which variant of the famous iPod is shown in this picture?

   (A) iPod Nano
   (B) iPod Shuffle
   (C) iPod Classic
   (D) iPod Touch

6. What is iCloud?
   (A) A free service from Apple
   (B) A new mobile phone from Apple
   (C) A new tablet from Apple
   (D) A new music player from Apple

7. This is a special icon with the feature designed to let you know when there's a notification waiting inside. What is the icon called?

   (A) Apple Icon
   (B) Badge App Icon
   (C) Notification Icon
   (D) Alert Icon

8. Which of the following are the two main menus of Windows 8?
   (A) All Apps and Titles
   (B) Start and Programs
   (C) Start and All Apps
   (D) All Apps and Programs

9. In which year did Windows 8 release?
   (A) 2012
   (B) 2008
   (C) 2019
   (D) 2013

10. Which version of Internet Explorer is featured in Windows 8.1?
   (A) Internet Explorer 8
   (B) Internet Explorer 9
   (C) Internet Explorer 10
   (D) Internet Explorer 11

11. What does the following image display?

   (A) The Home Screen of Windows 7
   (B) The Start Screen of Windows 8
   (C) The Apps Menu on the Ipad
   (D) The Charms Menu on Windows 8

12. What is the full form of GPS?
   (A) Global Positioning System
   (B) Global Packet System
   (C) Geo Positioning System
   (D) Geometrical Position System

13. Which of the following phones run on Android 4.4 Operating System?
   (A) Google Nexus 5
   (B) Google Nexus 4
   (C) Nokia Lumia 720
   (D) iPhone 5

14. Which of the following is NOT a version of the android operating system?
   (A) Red Hat
   (B) Jelly Bean
   (C) Ice Cream Sandwich
   (D) Kitkat

15. Which of the following is NOT an editing Windows 8 operating system?
   (A) Windows 8 Pro
   (B) Windows 8 Enterprise
   (C) Windows RT
   (D) Windows 8 Ultimate

16. Which is the version of the Windows Media Player released on July 22 2009 available for Windows 7 and Windows 8?
(A) Windows Media Player 12
(B) Windows Media Player 15
(C) Windows Media Player 11
(D) Windows Media Player 9 series

17. What is the name of the tablet from Microsoft?
(A) Microsoft Pad
(B) Microsoft LT
(C) Microsoft Tablet
(D) Microsoft Surface Pro 2

18. What is the name of the tablet launched by the Indian government?
(A) Sukhoi
(B) Prithvi
(C) Aakash
(D) DataWind

19. What is Sony's latest game console announced on February 2, 2021?
(A) PlayStation
(B) PlayStation 2
(C) PlayStation 4
(D) PlayStation 5

20. Which company is the manufacturer of Aakash tablet?
(A) Data Wind
(B) ISRO
(C) Microsoft
(D) Google

HOTS (ACHIEVERS SECTION)

21. You can open this application store from the start screen of Windows 8.1 to browse and download apps for cooking, sports, news, etc. Identify it.

(A) Skydrive
(B) Skype
(C) Windows store
(D) Downloadable store

22. Which of the following is the first Windows RT tablet developed by Nokia and released on November 21, 2013?
(A) Nokia lumia 2520
(B) Nokia lumia 743
(C) Nokia lumia 819
(D) Nokia lumia 143

23. Smartphones have gained immense popularity in the last few years. You can do almost everything on a smartphone that you used to do on desktop PCs. Which of the following tasks CANNOT be performed on smartphone?
(A) Surfing Internet
(B) Playing games
(C) Reading a CD
(D) Downloading music

24.  is an online file storage service by.
(A) Google
(B) Microsoft
(C) Yahoo
(D) Apple

25. Activity trackers are devices that monitor fitness activities such as distance travelled or run, calories consumed etc., to check your fitness level. They are examples of __________ technology.

(A) Cloud
(B) Wearable
(C) Real life
(D) Secret storage

1.	Ⓐ Ⓑ Ⓒ Ⓓ	6.	Ⓐ Ⓑ Ⓒ Ⓓ	11.	Ⓐ Ⓑ Ⓒ Ⓓ	16.	Ⓐ Ⓑ Ⓒ Ⓓ	21	Ⓐ Ⓑ Ⓒ Ⓓ
2.	Ⓐ Ⓑ Ⓒ Ⓓ	7.	Ⓐ Ⓑ Ⓒ Ⓓ	12.	Ⓐ Ⓑ Ⓒ Ⓓ	17.	Ⓐ Ⓑ Ⓒ Ⓓ	22	Ⓐ Ⓑ Ⓒ Ⓓ
3.	Ⓐ Ⓑ Ⓒ Ⓓ	8.	Ⓐ Ⓑ Ⓒ Ⓓ	13.	Ⓐ Ⓑ Ⓒ Ⓓ	18.	Ⓐ Ⓑ Ⓒ Ⓓ	23	Ⓐ Ⓑ Ⓒ Ⓓ
4.	Ⓐ Ⓑ Ⓒ Ⓓ	9.	Ⓐ Ⓑ Ⓒ Ⓓ	14.	Ⓐ Ⓑ Ⓒ Ⓓ	19.	Ⓐ Ⓑ Ⓒ Ⓓ	24	Ⓐ Ⓑ Ⓒ Ⓓ
5.	Ⓐ Ⓑ Ⓒ Ⓓ	10.	Ⓐ Ⓑ Ⓒ Ⓓ	15.	Ⓐ Ⓑ Ⓒ Ⓓ	20.	Ⓐ Ⓑ Ⓒ Ⓓ	25.	Ⓐ Ⓑ Ⓒ Ⓓ

LOGICAL REASONING

LEARNING OBJECTIVES

- ➤ Patterns
- ➤ Odd One Out
- ➤ Tips on Series
- ➤ Analogy
- ➤ Classification

- ➤ Letter to letter
- ➤ Ranking Based Problems
- ➤ Mirror Image
- ➤ Calendar
- ➤ Plane Figures

MULTIPLE CHOICE QUESTIONS

1. What are the next two shapes to complete the pattern?

(A) Circle, circle
(B) Triangle, circle
(C) Circle, triangle
(D) Square, circle

2. What are the next two shapes to complete the pattern?

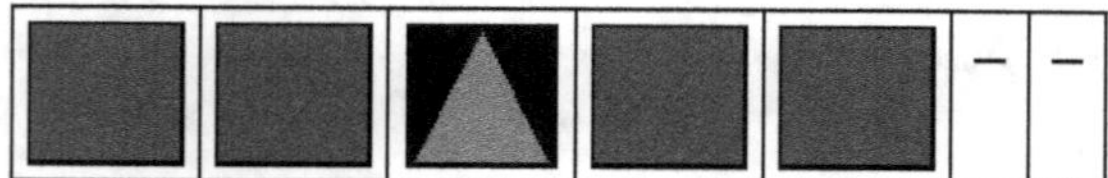

(A) Circle, circle
(B) Triangle, square
(C) Circle, triangle
(D) Square, circle

3. Find the number pattern in star A. The first point has a value of 3. Then look at star B. Use the same number pattern to figure out the value of the other points.

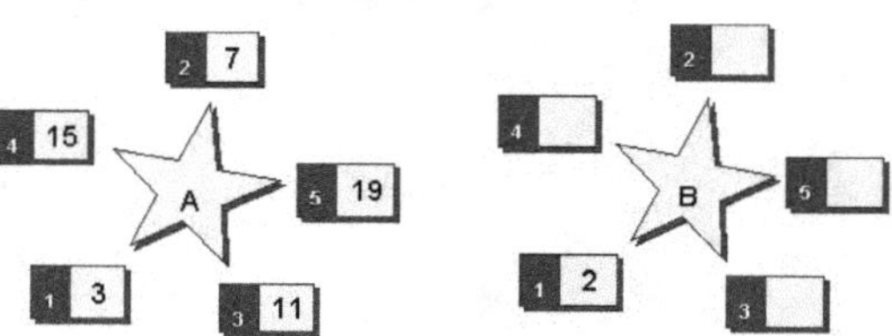

(A) 5, 7, 9, 18   (B) 4, 6, 8, 10
(C) 6, 10, 14, 18   (D) 10, 12, 14, 16

4. Find the odd one out.
(A) CD   (B) KL
(C) EF   (D) ON

5. Find the odd one out.
(A) AC   (B) TU
(C) MO   (D) XZ

6. Find the odd one out.
(A) POP   (B) BOB
(C) POT   (D) TOT

Directions (7-9): Find the next letter in the series given below.

7. C   D   E   F   G   ?
(A) K   (B) J
(C) I   (D) H

8. A   D   G   J   M   ?
   (A) O   (B) P
   (C) Q   (D) R

9. D   F   H   J   L   ?
   (A) O   (B) N
   (C) M   (D) P

10. Thick is related to Thin in the same way as Idle is related to ______.
    (A) Virtuous   (B) Business
    (C) Industrious   (D) Activity

11. Coherent is related to Consistent in the same way as Irate is related to
    (A) Unreasonable
    (B) Unhappy
    (C) Irritated
    (D) Angry

12. Claymore is related to Sword in the same way as Beretta is related to ______.
    (A) Club   (B) Axe
    (C) Knife   (D) Gun

Directions (13–15): Capital letters A to Z are given in the table below. Under each capital letter, a small letter is written which is to be used as a code for the capital letters.

Letter	A	B	C	D	E	F	G	H	I	J	K	L	M	N	O	P	Q	R	S	T	U	V	W	X	Y	Z
Code	n	z	o	y	p	x	q	w	r	a	s	b	v	c	t	d	u	e	f	m	g	l	h	k	i	j

Based on the table given above, write the codes for the following words.

13. UNIFIED
    (A) gcxrrpy   (B) gcrxrpy
    (C) qcrxrpy   (D) grcxpny

14. BMW
    (A) nvz   (B) lth
    (C) znv   (D) zvh

15. BRAIN
    (A) zenrc   (B) eznrc
    (C) zenre   (D) crrez

16. Some boys are sitting in a row. P is sitting fourteenth from the left and Q is seventh from the right. If there are four boys between P and Q, how many boys are there in the row?
    (A) 19   (B) 21
    (C) 23   (D) 25

17. Golu is 7 ranks ahead of Ankit in a class of 39. If Ankit's rank is seventeenth from the last, what is Golu's rank from the start?
    (A) 11th
    (B) 13th
    (C) 16th
    (D) 18th

18. Meetu is fourteenth from the right end in a row of 40 boys. What is his position from the left end?
    (A) 21th   (B) 24th
    (C) 25th   (D) 27th

19. Choose the alternative which closely resembles the mirror image of the given combination.
    TERMINATE
    (1) TƎᴙMINATƎ   (2) ƎTANIMᴙƎT
    (3) ƎTANIMᴙƎT   (4) ETANIMᴙƎT
    (A) 1
    (B) 2
    (C) 3
    (D) 4

20. Choose the alternative which closely resembles the mirror image of the given combination.
    BRISK
    (1) ꓘSIᴙB   (2) ꓘƧIRB
    (3) KƧIᴙB   (4) ꓘƧIᴙB
    (A) 1   (B) 2
    (C) 3   (D) 4

21. Choose the alternative which closely resembles the mirror image of the given combination.
    INFORMATIONS
    (1) INᖶOᴙMATIONƧ   (2) INꟻOᴙMATIONƧ
    (3) ƧNOITAMᴙOꟻNI   (4) ƧNOITAMᴙOꟻNI
    (A) 1   (B) 2
    (C) 3   (D) 4

22. If brushing : minutes : : sleeping : ?
    (A) Seconds
    (B) Hours
    (C) Days
    (C) Months
23. Find the odd one out.
    (A) 10/11/2001
    (B) 5/17/2001
    (C) 17/5/2001
    (D) 11/10/2001
24. AM refers to which part of the day?
    (A) Morning
    (B) Afternoon
    (C) Evening
    (D) Lunchtime
25. The Sun is at its peak at what time of the day?
    (A) Morning   (B) Noon
    (C) Evening   (D) Night
26. Moon shines brightly at __________.
    (A) Morning   (B) Noon
    (C) Evening   (D) Night
27. Noon time refers to
    (A) 12 pm   (B) 12 am
    (C) 11:55 pm   (D) 11:55 am
28. What is the difference between 9:30 am and 11:00 am?
    (A) 1 hour
    (B) 1 hour 15 minutes
    (C) 1 hour 30 minutes
    (D) 2 hours
29. What is the ideal lunch time?
    (A) 2:00 pm   (B) 5:00 pm
    (C) 8:00 am   (D) 8:00 pm
30. What shape is the tissue box?

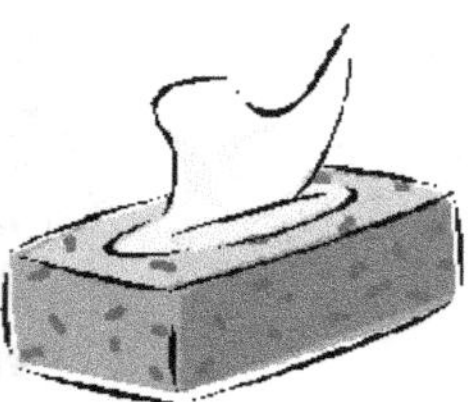

    (A) Triangle
    (B) Rectangle
    (C) Square
    (D) Circle
31. What shape is the STOP sign?

    (A) Hexagon
    (B) Octagon
    (C) Pentagon
    (D) Sphere
32. What shape is the globe?

    (A) Triangle
    (B) Square
    (C) Circle
    (D) Rectangle
33. What shapes are the buildings and the yield sign?

    (A) Rectangle and square
    (B) Rectangle and triangle
    (C) Cube and triangle
    (D) Rectangular pyramid and triangle

34. What shapes are used to make the house?

(A) Square, triangle, and rectangle
(B) Square, circle, and rectangle
(C) Square, triangle, and hexagon
(D) Square, triangle, and circle

35. What shape is the TV?

(A) Hexagon
(B) Square
(C) Triangle
(D) Rectangle

MODEL TEST PAPER

Mental Ability

1. Given that a and b are two different single digit numbers, find the values of a and b respectively.

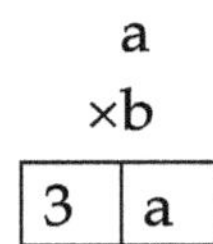

$$
\begin{array}{r}
a \\
\times b \\
\hline
\end{array}
$$

3	a

   (A) 5, 7 (B) 7, 5
   (C) 6, 6 (D) 4, 8

2. 5623 is 1623 more than _______ tens.
   (A) 724 (B) 7246
   (C) 400 (D) 4000

3. Megha drove from Town A to Town B and then to Town C. She then drove back to Town A from Town C. What was the total distance she travelled?

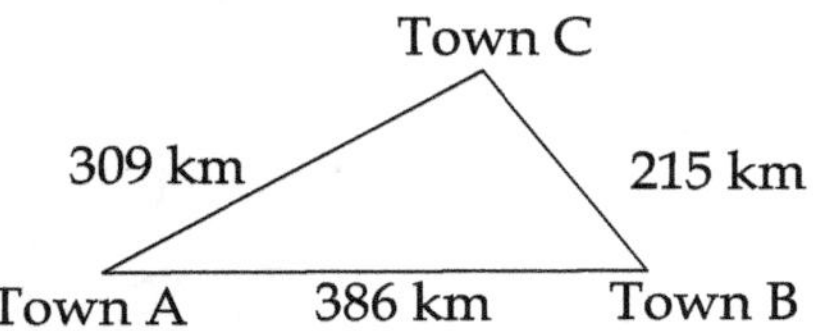

   (A) 650 km (B) 540 km
   (C) 910 km (D) 280 km

4. Sneha bought a chocolate and a cake. She gave the cashier two ₹500 notes and received ₹323 back. If the chocolate costs ₹68, what was the cost of the cake?
   (A) ₹582 (B) ₹509
   (C) ₹610 (D) ₹609

5. If I shade 2 more small rectangles in the given figure, what fraction of the figure will be unshaded?

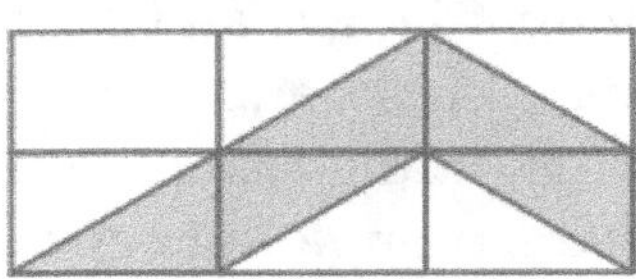

   (A) 1/4 (B) 1/2
   (C) 3/4 (D) 5/4

Logical and Analytical Reasoning

6. How many line segments are there in the given figure?

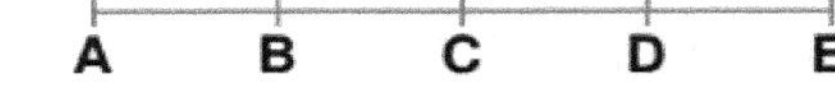

   (A) 12 (B) 14
   (C) 10 (D) 18

7. A "Happy Journey!" greeting was exchanged exactly once between two good friends. How many "Happy Journey!" greetings were exchanged among eight good friends?
   (A) 32 (B) 42
   (C) 38 (D) 28

8. Four runners took part in a 100 m race. Mohit: I was neither in the second place nor the last place. Aditya: I was faster than Mohit. Rohit: I was the first. Tanuj: I was slower than Mohit. Who stood last in the race?
   (A) Mohit (B) Aditya
   (C) Rohit (D) Tanuj

9. Find the odd one out.

   (A) 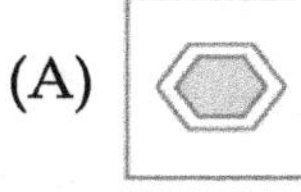 (B) 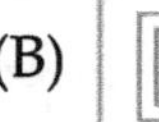

   (C)  (D) 

10. Which of the following figures is formed by using three circles and two squares together?

(A) 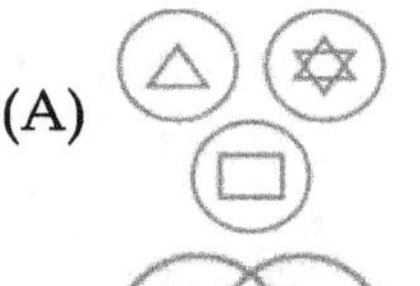

(B) 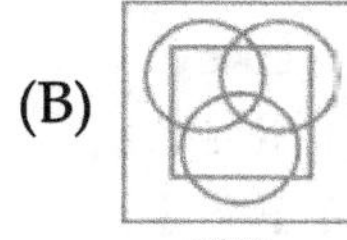

(C) 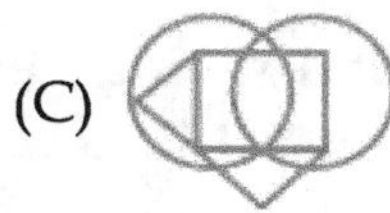

(D) 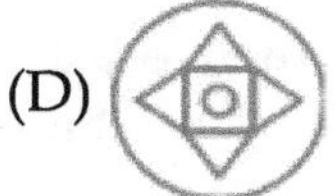

11. Find the word that cannot be made from the letters of the given word.
NEWSPAPER
(A) ERASE   (B) SPARE
(C) REPAIR   (D) RENEW

12. If 'Father' is called 'Mother', 'Mother' is called 'Sister', 'Sister' is called 'Brother', and 'Brother' is called 'Grandfather', then what is father's wife called?
(A) Father   (B) Sister
(C) Brother   (D) Grandfather

13. Find the figure from the options which is embedded in figure (X).

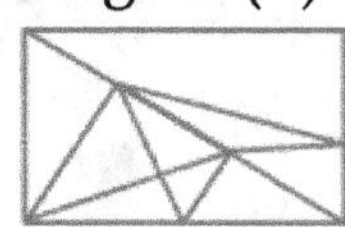

Fig. (X)

(A) 

(B) 

(C) 

(D) 

14. Find the missing number in the given series.

(A) 20   (B) 19
(C) 23   (D) 24

15. Figures (i) and (ii) are related to each other in some manner. Establish a similar relationship between figures (iii) and (iv) by selecting a suitable figure from the options.

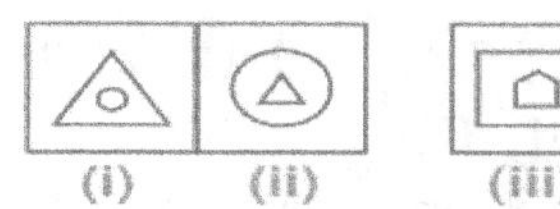

(A)    (B) 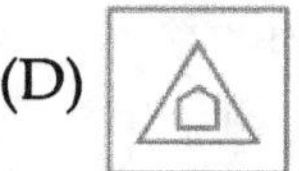

(C)   (D)

Computers & Information Technology

16. Which of the following is NOT a ready made shape in MS Paint of Windows 7?
(A) ⇨   (B) (small square icon)
(C) ☆   (D) (pentagon)

17. Creating an artificial environment to have a real life experience like walking in space without actually being in space is called ______.
(A) Virtual reality
(B) Multimedia
(C) Graphics
(D) Animation

18. Cutting and pasting a sentence is known as ______.
(A) Text editing
(B) Text formatting
(C) Indentation
(D) Text wrapping

19. Match the following MS Paint icons of Windows 7 with their uses.

(i) (icon)   (A) Draws a shape with any number of sides

(ii) (icon)   (B) Cancels the last operation

(iii) (icon)   (C) Helps to view picture full screen

(iv) (icon)   (D) Removes all portions that lay outside the selection

(A) (i)–(C), (ii)–(A), (iii)–(B), (iv)–(D)

(B) (i)–(D), (ii)–(C), (iii)–(B), (iv)–(A)

(C) (i)–(D), (ii)–(C), (iii)–(A), (iv)–(B)

(D) (i)–(A), (ii)–(C), (iii)–(B), (iv)–(D)

20. Which of the following is a cursor control device?

(A) Printer

(B) Scanner

(C) Trackball

(D) Microphone

21. You cannot connect to the internet through __________.

(A) 
(B) 
(C) 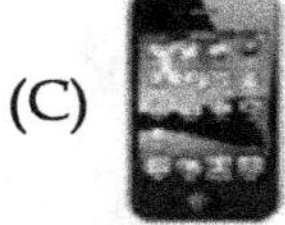
(D) 

22. Find the odd one out.

(A) 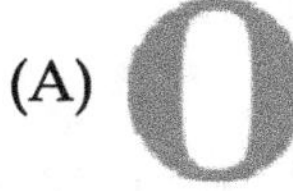
(B) 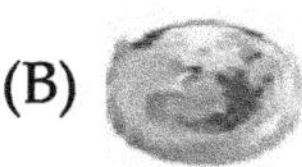
(C) 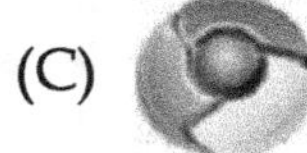
(D) 

23. Which of the following mouse pointer shapes is displayed when used for website links?

(A) 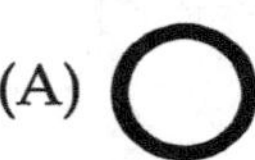
(B) 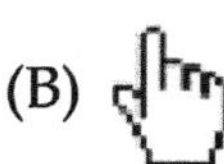
(C) 
(D) 

24. __________ in Windows 7 makes file organizing and searching easier.

(A) Jumplists

(B) Aerosnap

(C) Libraries

(D) Gadgets

25. In MS Paint of Windows 7, the ______ command changes the angle of an image.

(A) Bold

(B) Skew

(C) Resize

(D) Flip

26. I am used to talking and giving verbal commands to the computer. I am ______.

(A) 
(B) 
(C) 
(D) 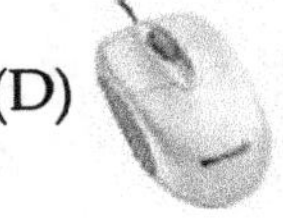

27. Select the incorrect match.

(A) LCD Monitor – 

(B) CRT Monitor – 

(C) Touchscreen – 

(D) Concept Keyboard –

28. Match the following.

Column-I	Column-II
(i) Occurs twice on the keyboard	(A) CapsLock
(ii) Use this key to jump six spaces on the screen	(B) Page Down
(iii) A toggle key	(C) Shift
(iv) One of the many Navigation Keys	(D) Tab

(A) (i)–(D), (ii)–(B), (iii)–(A), (iv)–(C)

(B) (i)–(D), (ii)–(A), (iii)–(B), (iv)–(C)

(C) (i)–(C), (ii)–(D), (iii)–(A), (iv)–(B)

(D) (i)–(C), (ii)–(A), (iii)–(B), (iv)–(D)

29. A scroll wheel is found on which of the following input devices?

(A)   (B)

(C)   (D)

30. The given image shows an example of __________.

(A) Monochrome monitor
(B) CRT monitor
(C) Keyboard
(D) Touchscreen

Achievers Section

31. When you start the computer, the first screen that you see is ________.
(A) Wallpaper   (B) Monitor
(C) Icons   (D) Desktop

32. Which one of the following is a tool of MS Paint?
(A) Colour   (B) Spray paint
(C) Paint Brush   (D) Square

33. What is similar to a copy machine, except that it creates a digital copy of the document instead of a paper copy?
(A) A website
(B) A scanner
(C) A copy machine
(D) A typewriter

34. To print a document, _______.
(A) Select the Print command and then select OK.
(B) Select the Ready Printer command then select OK.
(C) Type PRINT and then press Enter.
(D) Close the document, select the Print command, then select OK.

35. In Windows 7, when you press the Ctrl, Alt and Delete keys simultaneously, __________.

(A) the computer logs off
(B) the computer locks up
(C) Starts Task Manager
(D) All of these

Darken Your Choice with HB Pencil

1.	Ⓐ Ⓑ Ⓒ Ⓓ	8.	Ⓐ Ⓑ Ⓒ Ⓓ	15.	Ⓐ Ⓑ Ⓒ Ⓓ	22.	Ⓐ Ⓑ Ⓒ Ⓓ	29.	Ⓐ Ⓑ Ⓒ Ⓓ
2.	Ⓐ Ⓑ Ⓒ Ⓓ	9.	Ⓐ Ⓑ Ⓒ Ⓓ	16.	Ⓐ Ⓑ Ⓒ Ⓓ	23.	Ⓐ Ⓑ Ⓒ Ⓓ	30.	Ⓐ Ⓑ Ⓒ Ⓓ
3.	Ⓐ Ⓑ Ⓒ Ⓓ	10.	Ⓐ Ⓑ Ⓒ Ⓓ	17.	Ⓐ Ⓑ Ⓒ Ⓓ	24.	Ⓐ Ⓑ Ⓒ Ⓓ	31.	Ⓐ Ⓑ Ⓒ Ⓓ
4.	Ⓐ Ⓑ Ⓒ Ⓓ	11.	Ⓐ Ⓑ Ⓒ Ⓓ	18.	Ⓐ Ⓑ Ⓒ Ⓓ	25.	Ⓐ Ⓑ Ⓒ Ⓓ	32.	Ⓐ Ⓑ Ⓒ Ⓓ
5.	Ⓐ Ⓑ Ⓒ Ⓓ	12.	Ⓐ Ⓑ Ⓒ Ⓓ	19.	Ⓐ Ⓑ Ⓒ Ⓓ	26.	Ⓐ Ⓑ Ⓒ Ⓓ	33.	Ⓐ Ⓑ Ⓒ Ⓓ
6.	Ⓐ Ⓑ Ⓒ Ⓓ	13.	Ⓐ Ⓑ Ⓒ Ⓓ	20.	Ⓐ Ⓑ Ⓒ Ⓓ	27.	Ⓐ Ⓑ Ⓒ Ⓓ	34.	Ⓐ Ⓑ Ⓒ Ⓓ
7.	Ⓐ Ⓑ Ⓒ Ⓓ	14.	Ⓐ Ⓑ Ⓒ Ⓓ	21.	Ⓐ Ⓑ Ⓒ Ⓓ	28.	Ⓐ Ⓑ Ⓒ Ⓓ	35.	Ⓐ Ⓑ Ⓒ Ⓓ

HINTS AND SOLUTIONS

<table>
<tr><td colspan="10">1. NUMBERS</td></tr>
<tr><td colspan="10">Answer Key</td></tr>
</table>

1. (B)	2. (A)	3. (B)	4. (B)	5. (A)	6. (A)	7. (C)	8. (C)	9. (D)	10. (D)
11. (A)	12. (C)	13. (A)	14. (A)	15. (A)	16. (C)	17. (A)	18. (D)	19. (D)	20. (C)

HOTS (ACHIEVERS SECTION)

21. (A)	22. (D)	23. (D)	24. (A)	25. (C)

2. INPUT AND OUTPUT DEVICES

Answer Key

1. (B)	2. (C)	3. (B)	4. (A)	5. (B)	6. (C)	7. (B)	8. (C)	9. (A)	10. (B)
11. (A)	12. (C)	13. (A)	14. (C)	15. (B)	16. (B)	17. (C)	18. (C)	19. (C)	20. (B)

1. **(B)**

   Image shown in option (B) is of a trackball, which is a cursor control device. When the ball on holder is rotated by finger then the cursor on the screen also get moved in the same direction

4. **(A)**

   The unscrambled word is SCROLL WHEEL. A scroll wheel is found in mouse and is used for scrolling a document up or down.

6. **(C)**

   Tab key is used for providing space generally or for switching between various options in a dialog box.

7. **(B)**

   The image shown in option (B) is of scanner. It is used for capturing data from hard copy outputs and it converts them into digital form to store them in the computer.

9. **(A)**

   Scanner, trackball and joystick are input devices, whereas printer is an output device.

12. **(C)**

   A wireless mouse is a mouse without a wire, which means users need not to worry about the length of the cable and it can be handled very easily.

13. **(A)**

   Continuous stationery is long strip of paper, which is used for printing invoices. From the given options, only Dot Matrix printer provide support for continuous stationery. So, option (A) is correct.

15. (B)

Trackball is used to control the cursor. Microphone is used to enter audio data and headphone is used to listen to audio data. So, from the given options, only option (2) can be used to feed audio data in a computer.

16. (B)

A laptop is all in one computing machine. It supports a touchpad which is used in place of mouse to select and open items.

<table>
<tr><td colspan="5" align="center">HOTS (ACHIEVERS SECTION)</td></tr>
<tr><td>21. (C)</td><td>22. (C)</td><td>23. (A)</td><td>24. (A)</td><td>25. (C)</td></tr>
</table>

21. (C)

A magnetic stripe reader is a special type of input device. It reads the data stored in a strip band, which is generally found on back of smartcards. It then verifies the information read by it with the stored information.

22. (C)

As stated in the question, the device I consists of both printer (output device) and scanner (input device), so it is said to be an input and an output device, as it performs both the functions.

23. (A)

The unscrambled word is INKJET, which is a type of non-impact printer. So, option (A) is correct.

24. (A)

The image shown is of Magnetic Ink Character Reader, that reads the information on cheques which is printed with a special magnetized ink.

3. MS PAINT

Answer Key									
1. (A)	2. (D)	3. (A)	4. (A)	5. (A)	6. (B)	7. (B)	8. (D)	9. (C)	10. (B)
11. (C)	12. (C)	13. (C)	14. (C)	15. (D)	16. (A)	17. (D)	18. (B)	19. (B)	20. (A)
21. (C)	22. (C)	23. (A)	24. (A)	25. (D)					

<table>
<tr><td colspan="5" align="center">HOTS (ACHIEVERS SECTION)</td></tr>
<tr><td>26. (A)</td><td>27. (A)</td><td>28. (B)</td><td>29. (B)</td><td>30. (B)</td></tr>
</table>

4. INTRODUCTION TO INTERNET

Answer Key									
1. (C)	2. (B)	3. (C)	4. (D)	5. (B)	6. (C)	7. (A)	8. (C)	9. (C)	10. (A)
11. (A)	12. (B)	13. (A)	14. (D)	15. (C)	16. (D)	17. (C)	18. (C)	19. (A)	20. (D)

21. (C)	22. (B)	23. (A)	24. (C)	25. (B)

5. MS WORD

Answer Key

1. (C)	2. (D)	3. (B)	4. (C)	5. (D)	6. (B)	7. (A)	8. (D)	9. (A)	10. (B)
11. (B)	12. (D)	13. (D)	14. (B)	15. (C)	16. (C)	17. (B)	18. (B)	19. (A)	20. (B)

HOTS (ACHIEVERS SECTION)

21. (C)	22. (C)	23. (A)	24. (C)	25. (C)

6. GENERATIONS OF COMPUTER

Answer Key

1. (B)	2. (A)	3. (C)	4. (B)	5. (B)	6. (A)	7. (C)	8. (A)	9. (C)	10. (D)
11. (D)	12. (A)	13. (D)	14. (C)	15. (B)	16. (B)	17. (C)	18. (A)	19. (D)	20. (C)

HOTS (ACHIEVERS SECTION)

21. (B)	22. (B)	23. (C)	24. (D)	25. (A)

7. LATEST DEVELOPMENTS IN 'IT'

Answer Key

1. (B)	2. (D)	3. (D)	4. (B)	5. (B)	6. (A)	7. (B)	8. (C)	9. (A)	10. (D)
11. (B)	12. (A)	13. (A)	14. (A)	15. (D)	16. (A)	17. (D)	18. (C)	19. (D)	20. (A)

HOTS (ACHIEVERS SECTION)

21. (C)	22. (A)	23. (C)	24. (B)	25. (B)

Answer Key

1. (A)	2. (B)	3. (C)	4. (D)	5. (B)	6. (C)	7. (D)	8. (B)	9. (B)	10. (C)
11. (D)	12. (D)	13. (B)	14. (D)	15. (A)	16. (D)	17. (C)	18. (D)	19. (C)	20. (D)
21. (C)	22. (B)	23. (B)	24. (A)	25. (B)	26. (D)	27. (A)	28. (C)	29. (A)	30. (B)
31. (B)	32. (C)	33. (B)	34. (A)	35. (D)					

4. (D)

The two letters are consecutive in options A, B and C.

5. (B)

In options A, C and D, one letter is between two letters.

6. (C)

The two letters on either side of O are the same except in c.

7. (D)

C(+2)→D(+2)→E(+2)→F(+2)→G(+2)→H

8 (B)

A(3)→D(+3)→G(+3)→J(+3)→M(+3)→P

9. (B)

D(+2)→F(+2)→H(+2)→J(+2)→L(+2)→N

10. (C)

The words in each pair are antonyms of each other.

11. (D)

The words in each pair are synonyms.

12. (D)

First is a type of second.

13. (B)

U-g, N-c, l-r and so on. Choice B is the only option that has gcr.

14. (D)

B-z, M-v and W-h

15. (A)

B-z, R-e, A-n, l-r and N-c

16. (D)

Number of boys in the row = number of boys till P + number of boys between P and Q + number of boys including Q and those behind Q = 14 + 4 + 7 = 25.

17. (C)

Ankit is 17th from the last and Golu is 7 ranks ahead of Ankit. So, Golu is 24th from the last. Number of students ahead of Golu in rank = (39 – 24) = 15. So, Golu is 16th from the start.

18. (D)

Clearly, number of boys towards the Meetu's left = (40 – 14) = 26. So, Meetu is 27th from the left end.

MODEL TEST PAPER

Answer Key

1. (A)	2. (C)	3. (C)	4. (D)	5. (A)	6. (C)	7. (D)	8. (D)	9. (C)	10. (B)
11. (C)	12. (B)	13. (B)	14. (C)	15. (A)	16. (B)	17. (A)	18. (A)	19. (B)	20. (C)
21. (D)	22. (D)	23. (B)	24. (C)	25. (B)	26. (C)	27. (C)	28. (C)	29. (B)	30. (D)
31. (D)	32. (C)	33. (B)	34. (A)	35. (D)					

SAMPLE OMR ANSWER SHEET

1. STUDENT NAME (IN ENGLISH CAPITAL LETTERS ONLY)

Students must write and darken the respective circles completely using HB Pencil only. Othewise their Answer Sheets will not be evaluated.

PERSONAL DETAILS

2. SCHOOL CODE

3. CLASS

4. SECTION

5. ROLL NO.

6. QUESTION PAPER SET

A ○
B ○
C ○
D ○

7. MOBILE NUMBER

8. GENDER

MALE ○
FEMALE ○

9. STREAM
(Only for Class XI and XII Students)

MATHEMATICS ○
BIOLOGY ○
OTHERS ○

MARK YOUR ANSWERS

1.	Ⓐ Ⓑ Ⓒ Ⓓ	26.	Ⓐ Ⓑ Ⓒ Ⓓ
2.	Ⓐ Ⓑ Ⓒ Ⓓ	27.	Ⓐ Ⓑ Ⓒ Ⓓ
3.	Ⓐ Ⓑ Ⓒ Ⓓ	28.	Ⓐ Ⓑ Ⓒ Ⓓ
4.	Ⓐ Ⓑ Ⓒ Ⓓ	29.	Ⓐ Ⓑ Ⓒ Ⓓ
5.	Ⓐ Ⓑ Ⓒ Ⓓ	30.	Ⓐ Ⓑ Ⓒ Ⓓ
6.	Ⓐ Ⓑ Ⓒ Ⓓ	31.	Ⓐ Ⓑ Ⓒ Ⓓ
7.	Ⓐ Ⓑ Ⓒ Ⓓ	32.	Ⓐ Ⓑ Ⓒ Ⓓ
8.	Ⓐ Ⓑ Ⓒ Ⓓ	33.	Ⓐ Ⓑ Ⓒ Ⓓ
9.	Ⓐ Ⓑ Ⓒ Ⓓ	34.	Ⓐ Ⓑ Ⓒ Ⓓ
10.	Ⓐ Ⓑ Ⓒ Ⓓ	35.	Ⓐ Ⓑ Ⓒ Ⓓ
11.	Ⓐ Ⓑ Ⓒ Ⓓ	36.	Ⓐ Ⓑ Ⓒ Ⓓ
12.	Ⓐ Ⓑ Ⓒ Ⓓ	37.	Ⓐ Ⓑ Ⓒ Ⓓ
13.	Ⓐ Ⓑ Ⓒ Ⓓ	38.	Ⓐ Ⓑ Ⓒ Ⓓ
14.	Ⓐ Ⓑ Ⓒ Ⓓ	39.	Ⓐ Ⓑ Ⓒ Ⓓ
15.	Ⓐ Ⓑ Ⓒ Ⓓ	40.	Ⓐ Ⓑ Ⓒ Ⓓ
16.	Ⓐ Ⓑ Ⓒ Ⓓ	41.	Ⓐ Ⓑ Ⓒ Ⓓ
17.	Ⓐ Ⓑ Ⓒ Ⓓ	42.	Ⓐ Ⓑ Ⓒ Ⓓ
18.	Ⓐ Ⓑ Ⓒ Ⓓ	43.	Ⓐ Ⓑ Ⓒ Ⓓ
19.	Ⓐ Ⓑ Ⓒ Ⓓ	44.	Ⓐ Ⓑ Ⓒ Ⓓ
20.	Ⓐ Ⓑ Ⓒ Ⓓ	45.	Ⓐ Ⓑ Ⓒ Ⓓ
21.	Ⓐ Ⓑ Ⓒ Ⓓ	46.	Ⓐ Ⓑ Ⓒ Ⓓ
22.	Ⓐ Ⓑ Ⓒ Ⓓ	47.	Ⓐ Ⓑ Ⓒ Ⓓ
23.	Ⓐ Ⓑ Ⓒ Ⓓ	48.	Ⓐ Ⓑ Ⓒ Ⓓ
24.	Ⓐ Ⓑ Ⓒ Ⓓ	49.	Ⓐ Ⓑ Ⓒ Ⓓ
25.	Ⓐ Ⓑ Ⓒ Ⓓ	50.	Ⓐ Ⓑ Ⓒ Ⓓ

Signature of the Student & Date of Examination

Signature of the Invigilator & Date of Examination

V&S Publishers, F-2/16 Ansari Road, Daryaganj, New Delhi-110002, ☎ 011-23240026-27
✉ info@vspublishers.com, 🌐 www.vspublishers.com